STARTERS

Journeys

Kay Woodward

A+

First published in 2004 by Hodder Wayland,
an imprint of Hodder Children's Books,
338 Euston Road, London NW1 3BH

Language consultant: Andrew Burrell
Subject consultant: John Lace
Design: Perry Tate Design
Picture research: Glass Onion Pictures

Published in the United States by Smart Apple Media
1980 Lookout Drive, North Mankato, Minnesota 56003

Library of Congress Cataloging-in-Publication Data

Woodward, Kay.
Journeys / Kay Woodward.
p. cm. — (Starters)
ISBN 1-58340-566-6
1. Travel—Juvenile literature. [1. Travel.] I. Title. II. Series.

G175.W67 2004
910'.2'02—dc22   2003070368

9 8 7 6 5 4 3 2 1

The publishers would like to thank the following for allowing us to reproduce their
pictures in this book: Angela Hampton / Family Life Picture Library; 6, 17 (bottom
right), 21 (top) / Corbis; contents page, 4 (top), 5 (top), 7 (top), 9, 10, 11 (bottom),
12, 13, 14, 15, 16 (middle), 17 (top), 18 (top), 19, 20, 21 (bottom), 22 (top), 23
(bottom) / Getty Images; 4 (bottom), 23 (top) / Hodder Wayland Picture Library; title
page, 5 (bottom), 7 (bottom), 8, 11 (top) / Encompass Graphics Ltd; 16 (top and
bottom), 17 (middle) / Zul Mukhida, Chapel Studios; 18 (bottom), 22 (bottom)

Contents

Going on a journey

When you go on a journey, you travel from one place to another. Journeys happen for many reasons.

You might go on a journey to school or to a birthday party.

You might visit friends, or go on a vacation to the beach.

Different journeys
need different kinds of
transportation.
Before you leave,
it's important
to decide how
you will
travel.

Near and far

Some journeys take you just around the corner or to the end of the street. For these short journeys, walking is often the easiest way to travel.

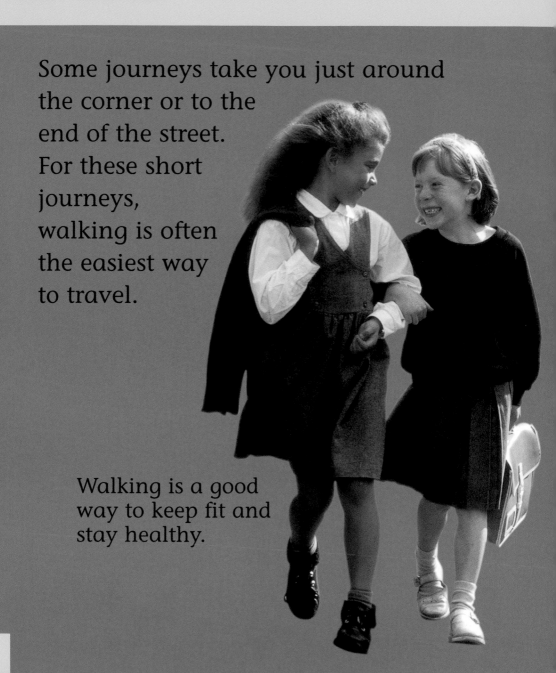

Walking is a good way to keep fit and stay healthy.

Bicycles and scooters
are ideal for longer
journeys—they allow
you to move
more quickly.

Many roads
have bike paths
beside them,
made especially
for people riding
bicycles and
scooters.

7

Wheels go around

People travel in cars when it is too far to walk, or when they want to get somewhere *quickly*.

With a full tank of gas, a car can travel a long way.

8

Sometimes a journey by car can take a long time, especially when the roads are busy.

When there is too much traffic on the road, cars travel very *s l o w l y*.

Traveling together

Buses can carry lots of people at the same time. A public city bus makes the same short journey again and again, picking up and dropping off passengers at bus stops along the way.

Students wait at bus stops until a school bus arrives to pick them up.

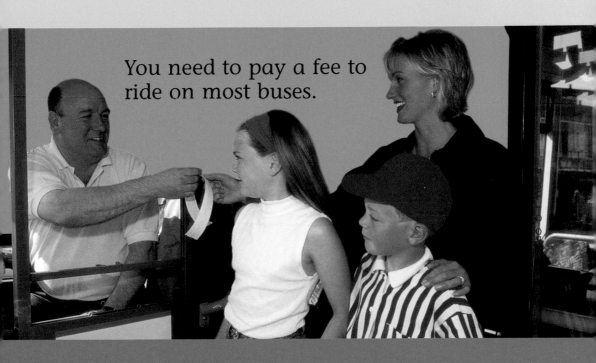

You need to pay a fee to ride on most buses.

Some buses have televisions, snacks, and bathrooms on board to make longer journeys more relaxing.

Along the tracks

Trains have lots of passenger cars so they can carry hundreds of people at once.

They **speed** along railroad tracks, taking passengers through valleys and tunnels, across bridges, and over hills.

In large cities, people travel on underground trains. These can go faster than the cars and buses on the busy roads above.

This train takes people from England to France through a tunnel under the ocean floor!

Up and away

Airplanes *soar* through the sky, flying quickly over land and sea. They take passengers on journeys all over the world.

Airplanes can travel halfway around the world in less than a day!

There is only one vehicle that can travel faster than an airplane—a space shuttle! Rockets are used to push space shuttles up into the sky until they are **HIGH** above Earth.

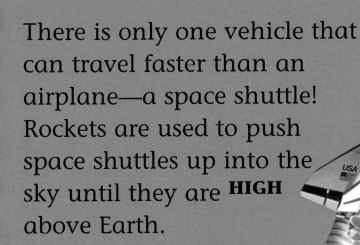

Very few people travel by space shuttle now, but maybe you will some day!

Time to pack

Once you have decided where to go and how to travel, there is one more decision to make: What should you take on your journey?

A map will help you find the way.

Bring a snack so you don't get hungry.

You can use a camera to take pictures of what you see.

If you are going on vacation, you might need a swimsuit, sunscreen,

sunglasses,

and a hat.

You'll also need a suitcase to pack them in.

On the way

During a journey, there's always something new to look at. One journey might take you past hotels, beaches, and  theme parks. Another might carry you past mountains, lakes, and castles.

Sometimes people need to take a break during a journey. Drivers need to rest, people need to go to the bathroom, and cars need to be filled up with gas. Passengers might even change to a different kind of transportation.

This ferry is carrying cars across the water.

Getting there

At the end of a journey, it feels good to stretch and yawn. Then it's time to unpack, look around, and have fun!

If you're visiting friends, you can laugh, talk, and play together.

At the beach, you can
paddle, swim, build
sandcastles, and eat
ice cream.

In a different country,
you might learn
how other
people live.

21

Home again!

Most journeys mean that people travel in two directions—going away and coming home again.

It's exciting to visit friends and see new places. You might feel sad when it's time to say good-bye.

But after a long,
tiring journey, home
is the best place in
the world to be!

Glossary and index

Bike path A path beside a road or in the countryside that is made especially for people riding bicycles. 7

Gas A liquid that is burned to make a car's engine work. 8, 19

Map A small drawing of a town, a country, or the world. 16

Passenger A person who travels in a vehicle but is not the driver. 10, 12, 14, 19

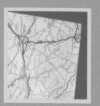

Passenger car The part of a train where lots of people can sit. 12

Space shuttle A vehicle used for traveling in space. 15

Traffic Vehicles traveling along the road. 9

Transportation Vehicles that can move people and things from one place to another. 5